Reach
HIGHER

Practice Book

NATIONAL
GEOGRAPHIC
LEARNING

Australia · Brazil · Mexico · Singapore · United Kingdom · United States

National Geographic Learning,
a Cengage Company

Reach Higher Practice Book 2A

Publisher, Content-based English: Erik Gundersen

Associate Director, R&D: Barnaby Pelter

Senior Development Editors:
  Jacqueline Eu
  Ranjini Fonseka
  Kelsey Zhang

Development Editor: Rayne Ngoi

Director of Global Marketing: Ian Martin

Heads of Regional Marketing:
  Charlotte Ellis (Europe, Middle East and Africa)
  Kiel Hamm (Asia)
  Irina Pereyra (Latin America)

Product Marketing Manager: David Spain

Senior Production Controller: Tan Jin Hock

Senior Media Researcher (Covers): Leila Hishmeh

Senior Designer: Lisa Trager

Director, Operations: Jason Seigel

Operations Support:
  Rebecca Barbush
  Drew Robertson
  Caroline Stephenson
  Nicholas Yeaton

Manufacturing Planner: Mary Beth Hennebury

Publishing Consultancy and Composition:
  MPS North America LLC

For permission to use material from this text or product,
submit all requests online at **cengage.com/permissions**
Further permissions questions can be emailed to
permissionrequest@cengage.com

ISBN-13: 978-0-357-36682-0

National Geographic Learning
200 Pier Four Blvd
Boston, MA 02210
USA

Locate your local office at **international.cengage.com/region**

Visit National Geographic Learning online at **ELTNGL.com**
Visit our corporate website at **www.cengage.com**

Printed in the United States of America
Print Number: 10   Print Year: 2023

Contents

Unit 3: Water for Everyone

Unit 4: Lend a Hand

Unit Concept Map

Hello, Neighbor!

Make a concept map with the answers to the Big Question:
What is a community?

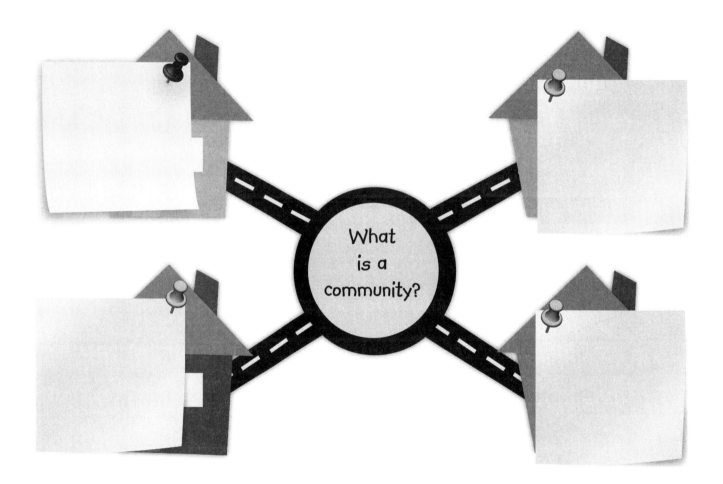

Name _____ Date _____

Character

Make a character map for Maria and Vera from the song
"Our Hometown Workers."

Character	What does the character do?	Where does the character work?

Share your character map with a partner.

Grammar

On the Job

Grammar Rules Nouns

A **noun** names a person, a place, or a thing.

Person	Place	Thing
cousin	park	flower
girl	garden	smile

Categorize the nouns as people, places or things.

My <u>uncle</u> takes me to his <u>shop</u>. He fixes <u>cars</u> in the <u>garage</u>. Our <u>neighbor</u> works there, too. I want to help, so I bring them the <u>tools</u> that they need. What a fun <u>job</u>!

Nouns		
Person	**Place**	**Thing**
uncle	_____	_____
_____	_____	_____
_____	_____	_____

Use three of the nouns above. Tell a partner something about you.

Name _____ Date _____

"Li Min's Community"

Listen as your teacher reads. Follow with your finger.

1 Li Min's parents go to work. Li Min will spend the day with her grandmother in their community.

2 First, they go to the community center. Then, they go to a market. Li Min gets a meat sandwich from Mr. Wu. They also buy some vegetables from Mrs. Chen. Finally, they stop at Dad's restaurant for some dumplings.

3 They walk some more and shop some more. Then, it's time to go home. Li Min really loves her community.

Name _____   Date _____

A Walk in the Park

Grammar Rules Plural Nouns

	Singular	Plural
Add **-s** to most nouns.	game	game**s**
Add **-es** to nouns that end in **x**, **ch**, **sh**, **ss**, **z**, and sometimes **o**.	box	box**es**
For nouns that end in **-y**, change the **y** to **i** and then add **-es**.	party	part**ies**

Read the paragraph and make the nouns plural.

Today, Marisa and I walked to the park. Marisa wanted to

play on the ___*swings*___ . Then we sat on the _____ to
            (swing)   (bench)

eat our _____ . I brought _____ to share. Then our
          (snack)   (strawberry)

_____ came. We played under the blue _____ for
  (friend)   (sky)

hours. What a great day!

 Pick two plural nouns from above and write new sentences. Read them to a partner.

Name _____ Date _____

"Li Min's Community"

Make a character map for the people in "Li Min's Community."

Character	What does the character do?	Where does the character work?
Li Min's father	He is a cook.	He works in a restaurant.
Li Min's mother	She is a nurse.	
Mr. Wu		He works in a food stall.

 Use your character map to describe the characters in "Li Min's Community" to a partner.

Three-Letter Blends: *scr, str*

<u>scr</u>ub

<u>str</u>eam

Circle the sounds at the beginning of each word.

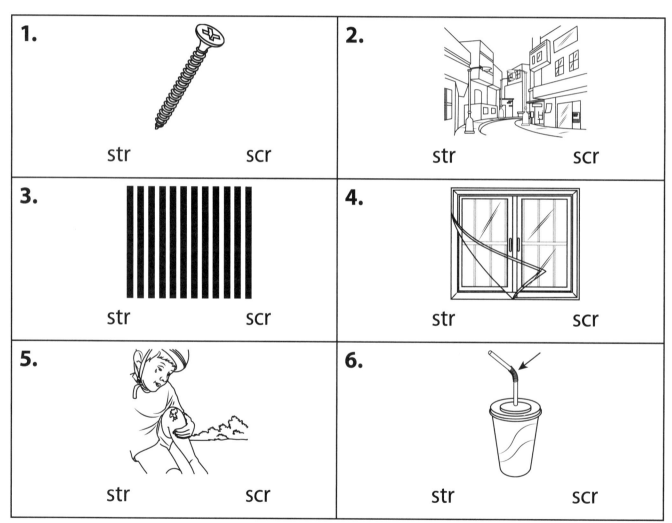

1.	str scr
2.	str scr
3.	str scr
4.	str scr
5.	str scr
6.	str scr

Work with a partner. Take turns reading the sentence and pointing to the objects.

Find a straw, a screw, a screen, and a street.

Fluency

"Li Min's Community"

Use this passage to practice reading with proper intonation.

First we go to our community center.   7

Grandma meets her friends at the center.   14

They like to exercise.   18

From "Li Min's Community," page 17

Intonation

| B | ☐ Does not change pitch. | | A | ☐ Changes pitch to match some of the content. |
| I | ☐ Changes pitch, but does not match content. | | AH | ☐ Changes pitch to match all of the content. |

Accuracy and Rate Formula

Use the formula to measure a reader's accuracy and rate while reading aloud.

$$\underset{\substack{\text{words attempted} \\ \text{in one minute}}}{\text{_____}} - \underset{\substack{\text{number of errors}}}{\text{_____}} = \underset{\substack{\text{words correct per minute} \\ \text{(wcpm)}}}{\text{_____}}$$

"Working Her Way Around the World"

Fill out the prediction chart as you read.

What I know about Annie Griffiths's job	What I think I will learn

Tell a partner about a new job you learned about.

Name _____   Date _____

Compare Genres

Make a comparison chart to show how realistic fiction and a photo-essay are different.

Realistic fiction	Photo-essay
• tells about things that could really happen	• uses photographs and text to tell about a topic

Take turns with a partner. Give information about a story or a photo-essay.

Grammar

The Make-It-Plural Game

1. Play with a partner.

2. Spin the spinner.

3. Change the noun to a plural noun. Say a sentence using the plural noun.

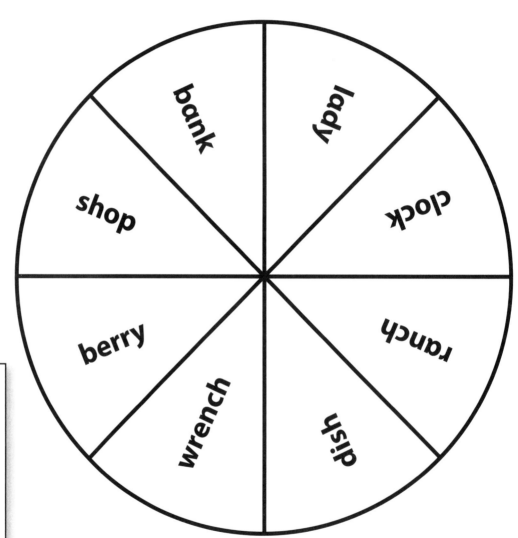

Make a Spinner

1. Place one loop of a paper clip over the center of the circle.

2. Push a sharp pencil through the loop and the paper.

3. Spin the paper clip around the pencil.

Name _____ Date _____

Our Community

Make a details cluster to tell about places in your community.

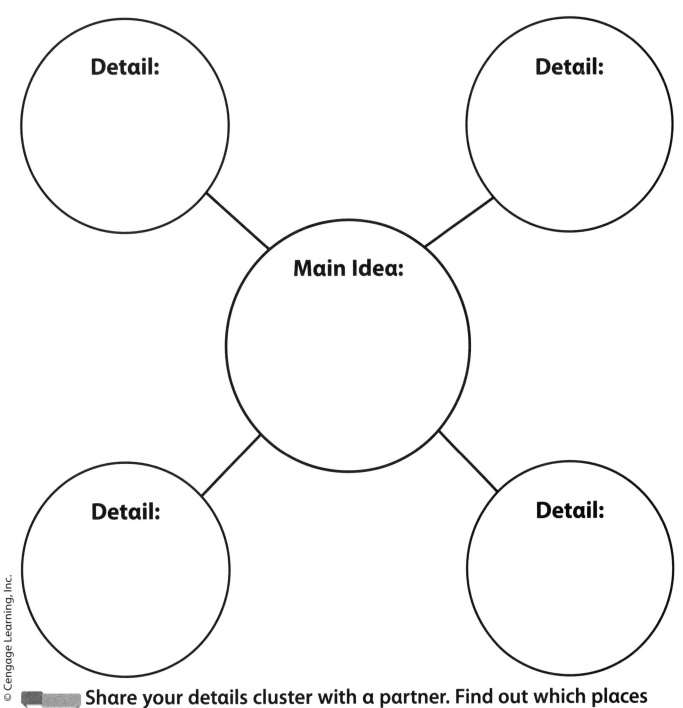

Detail:

Detail:

Main Idea:

Detail:

Detail:

Share your details cluster with a partner. Find out which places you both enjoy in your community.

Grammar

Places To Go

Grammar: Proper Nouns

- A **common noun** names a person, place, or thing.
  Example: *hospital*

- A **proper noun** names a specific person, place, or thing. Each proper noun begins with a **capital letter**.
  Example: *Mercy Hospital*

Categorize the nouns as common nouns or proper nouns.

Ezra wants to go to the park. First, he must do his homework. He must read *Charlotte's Web.* He can find this book at Oak Public Library. The library is on King Street.

Common nouns	Proper nouns
park	Ezra

Tell a partner the name of the street, city, and state where you live. Use proper nouns.

"Be My Neighbor"

Listen as your teacher reads. Follow with your finger.

1  A neighborhood is the place where you live. Some neighborhoods are large. Others are small.

2  Neighborhoods have places to play and shop. They have places to work and celebrate.

3  Neighbors share the place where they live. It's the place you call home.

© Cengage Learning, Inc.

Grammar

Make-It-Possessive Game

Grammar Rules Possessive Nouns

Make a noun possessive by adding an **apostrophe** (') plus **-s** to the end. Example: *Sam**'s***

1. **Play with a partner.**

2. **Flip a coin.**

 Move 1 space.

 Move 2 spaces.

3. **Change the noun to a possessive noun. Say a sentence using the possessive noun.**

4. **The player who finishes first wins.**

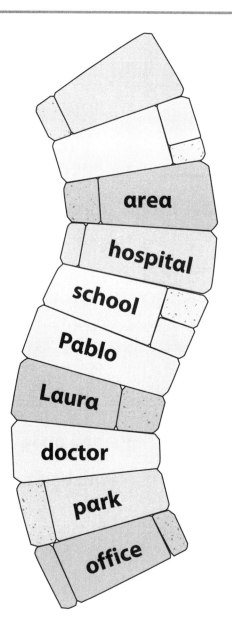

area

hospital

school

Pablo

Laura

doctor

park

office

Vocabulary Bingo

Play Bingo using the Key Words from this unit.

Name _____   Date _____

"Be My Neighbor"

Make a details cluster for "Be My Neighbor." Look for details that tell more about the main idea.

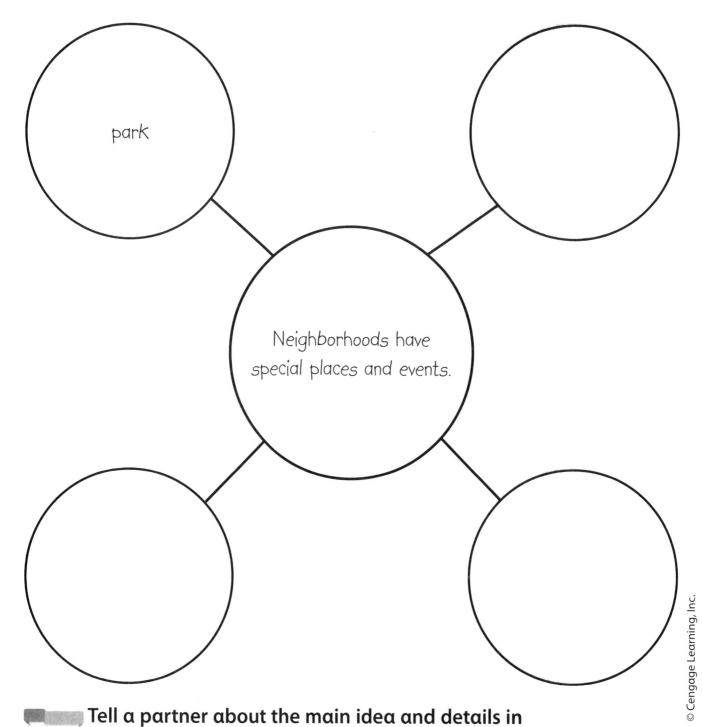

park

Neighborhoods have special places and events.

Tell a partner about the main idea and details in "Be My Neighbor."

Phonics Practice

Three-Letter Blends: *spl, spr*

splash

spray

Draw a line from the correct blend to the rest of the word. Write the word on the line.

1. spl out spr _____	**2.** spl int spr _____
3. spl its spr _____	**4.** spl ing spr _____
5. spl ash spr _____	**6.** spl ead spr _____

Work with a partner. Take turns reading the sentence and pointing to the objects.

Find a splash, a splint, and a sprout.

Unit 1 | Hello, Neighbor!

Fluency

"Be My Neighbor"

Use this passage to practice reading with proper phrasing.

Most neighborhoods have markets, shopping malls,   6

or grocery stores. Families can buy what they need   15

at these places.   18

From "Be My Neighbor," page 51

Phrasing

[B] ☐ Rarely pauses while reading the text.   [A] ☐ Frequently pauses at appropriate points in the text.

[I] ☐ Occasionally pauses while reading the text.   [AH] ☐ Consistently pauses at all appropriate points in the text.

Accuracy and Rate Formula

Use the formula to measure a reader's accuracy and rate while reading aloud.

$$\underline{\hspace{3cm}} - \underline{\hspace{3cm}} = \underline{\hspace{3cm}}$$

words attempted   number of errors   words corrected per
in one minute   minute (wcpm)

Name _____   Date _____

"My Favorite Place"

Fill out the reflection journal as you read "My Favorite Place."

Page	My questions	The answers

Discuss what you wrote in your reflection journal with your teacher.

Compare Media

Use the comparison chart to compare "Be My Neighbor" and "My Favorite Place."

	Photo-essay	Internet bulletin board
has photos	✓	✓
has captions		
has more than one writer		
gives facts		
asks and answers questions		
lets people share ideas and communicate		

Take turns with a partner. Ask each other questions about a photo-essay or an Internet bulletin board.

Grammar

A Day in the Park

Grammar Rules Proper and Possessive Nouns

- A **proper noun** names a specific person, place, or thing. Example: *Texas*
- Some titles of people begin with a **capital letter** and end with a **period**. Example: *Dr.*
- A **possessive noun** names an owner. Example: *Jackson's*

Underline the proper nouns and write them in the chart. Then make each proper noun possessive.

Mrs. Preston lives in a neighborhood called Grandview. Her home is on Maple Street. Adam Preston is her son. We go to the same school. He is on my soccer team, too. Mr. Mohr is our coach.

Proper nouns	Proper possessive nouns
Mrs. Preston	Mrs. Preston's

 Write a sentence with a proper noun and a proper possessive noun. Read your sentence to a partner.

Writing Project

Ideas

Writing is well developed when the message is clear and interesting to the reader. It is supported by details that show the writer knows the topic well.

	Is the message clear and focused?	Do the details show the writer knows the topic?
4 Wow!	❑ All of the writing is clear and focused.	❑ All the details tell about the topic. ❑ The writer knows the topic well.
3 Ahh.	❑ Most of the writing is clear and focused.	❑ Most of the details are about the topic. ❑ The writer knows the topic fairly well.
2 Hmm.	❑ Some of the writing is not clear. The writing lacks some focus.	❑ Some details are about the topic. ❑ The writer doesn't know the topic well.
1 Huh?	❑ The writing is not clear or focused.	❑ Many details are not about the topic. ❑ The writer does not know the topic.

Writing Project

Details Cluster

Complete the details cluster for your photo-essay.

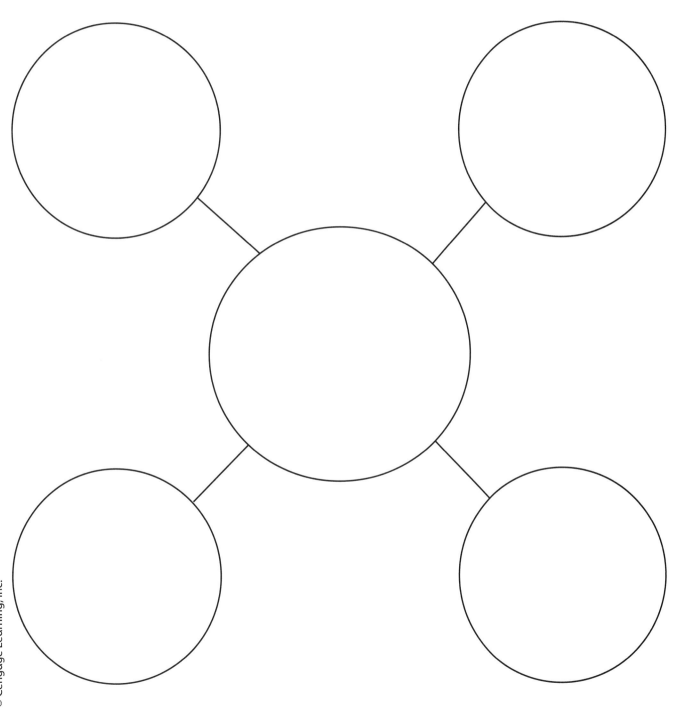

Writing Project

Revise

Use revision marks to make changes to this paragraph. Look for:

- **a topic sentence**
- **relevant details**

Revision Marks	
∧	Add
℘	Take out
⟲	Move to here

Jack goes to the senior center every weekend. He plays games with

Mr. Garcia. He takes walks with Mrs. Tran. He wears shorts in the summer. Jack

always looks forward to helping at the senior center! He likes to swim, too.

Edit and Proofread

Use revision marks to edit and
proofread this paragraph. Look for:

- correct spelling of regular plural nouns
- correct form of irregular plural nouns
- capitalization of proper nouns

Revision Marks	
∧	Add
℉	Take out
⬭⤴	Move to here
⬭	Check spelling
≡	Capitalize

Anna garcia is a very special person. She works in the

animal shelter on main Street. She takes care of all the dog and

cats. Sometimes she takes care of rabbits and mouses, too!

Every day she brushes the dogs. They give her lots of kisss.

Unit Concept Map

Staying Alive

Make a concept map with the answers to the Big Question:
What does it take to survive?

What does it take to survive?

Name __Ella__

Date _____

The Nature Walk

Use a beginning-middle-end chart to make a story map about a nature walk.

Beginning:

How does the story start?

FOrSt
Pablo
fand
Caterpillar

Middle:

What happens next in the story?

than

he Pot

da caterpillar
an jar
and lok

End:

How does the story end?

than
da
caterpillar
torn
to

Baterfllay than Pablo open da jar

Share your beginning-middle-end chart with a partner.

Grammar

At the Park

Grammar Rules Action Verbs

An **action verb** tells what a person, animal, or thing does.

> Examples: *The boy* **runs**.   *His parents* **talk**.

Add an **–s** to most action verbs to tell what one person, animal, or thing does.

> Example: *Our dog* **chases** *squirrels*.

Do not add **–s** to tell what two or more people, animals, or things do.

> Example: *The squirrels* **climb** *the tree*.

**Write the correct form of the verb to complete each sentence.
Then read the sentence to a partner.**

1. see   The girl ____*sees*____ a pair of robins.

2. build   The birds _____ a nest.

3. lay   The mother robin _____ three eggs.

4. open   The eggs _____ in two weeks.

5. feed   The parents _____ their hungry babies.

6. cheep   A hungry baby robin _____ .

7. swallow   The baby robin _____ a worm.

8. grow   The baby robins _____ quickly.

"Twilight Hunt"

Listen as your teacher reads. Follow with your finger.

The Screech Owl's babies are hungry. It begins to hunt for food.

It looks for movements and listens for sounds. It sees many creatures, but it cannot catch them.

Finally, it catches a Luna Moth. A Great Horned Owl is watching the Screech Owl.

The Screech Owl hides on a tree. It waits. Then it takes the food home to its babies.

Grammar

What Can I Do? What Might I Find?

Grammar Rules Helping Verbs

Can, **may**, and **might** are **helping verbs**. Use them with action verbs.

Examples: *Mike **can** swim like a fish.*

*He **may** go to the pool tomorrow.*

*I **might** swim with him, too.*

Read the sentences below and write your answers.

1. Can you hop like a katydid? Can you jump like a frog? Write about something you are able to do.

   I _____

   _____

2. Pretend you are walking in the woods. Write about something that is possible to see. Use the helping verb **may**.

   I _____

   _____

3. Imagine you are an owl hunting for food. Write a sentence about what you might find.

   I _____

   _____

   ▬▬▬ **Tell a partner which story event was your favorite and why.**

© Cengage Learning, Inc.

Reread and Retell

"Twilight Hunt"

Use a beginning-middle-end chart to show the plot of "Twilight Hunt."

Beginning:

Screech Owl goes on a hunt. She must find food for her babies.

Middle:

End:

Use your beginning-middle-end chart to tell a partner about "Twilight Hunt."

Phonics Practice

Digraphs: *ph, th, qu*

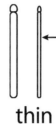

p̲hone   t̲hin   q̲ueen

Draw a line from the correct digraph to the rest of the word. Write the word on the line.

1.	ph th orn qu _____	**2.** ph th one qu _____
3.	ph th iet qu _____	**4.** ph th irty qu _____
5.	ph th oto qu _____	**6.** ph th estion qu _____

Work with a partner. Take turns asking and answering the question.

Can you ask a quiet question?

Name _____ Date _____

"Twilight Hunt"

Use this passage to practice reading with proper expression.

Sensing danger, the Screech Owl swoops to land.   8

With feathers pulled tight, the   13

Screech Owl has disappeared.   17

So, the Great Horned Owl flies on.   24

From "Twilight Hunt," pages 92–93

Expression

B ☐ Does not read with feeling.   A ☐ Reads with appropriate feeling for most content.

I ☐ Reads with some feeling, but does not match content.   AH ☐ Read with appropriate feeling for all content.

Accuracy and Rate Formula

Use the formula to measure a reader's accuracy and rate while reading aloud.

_____ − _____ = _____
words attempted   number of errors   words corrected per
in one minute   minute (wcpm)

Hide and Seek

Complete a K-W-L-Q chart as you read "Hide and Seek."

K What I know	W What I want to learn	L What I learned	Q What I still want to learn

Share ideas with a partner. Talk about which animal is your favorite and why.

Respond and Extend

Compare Genres

Compare the story and the science article, using the Venn diagram below.

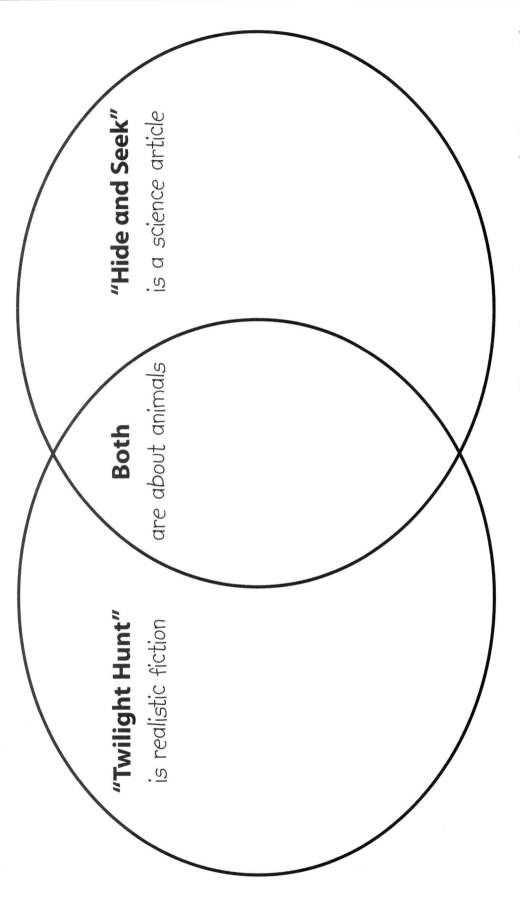

"Hide and Seek"
is a science article

Both
are about animals

"Twilight Hunt"
is realistic fiction

Share your diagram with a partner. Take turns talking about the story and science article.

Grammar

Roll a Verb

Grammar Rules **Action and Helping Verbs**

For **Action Verbs**
- Use **-s** at the end of an action verb if the subject is **he**, **she**, or **it**.
- Do not use **-s** for **I**, **you**, **we**, or **they**.

For **Action Verbs** with **Helping Verbs**
- A **helping verb** comes before the **main verb**.

Use a die to play this game.

1. **Play with a partner. Roll the die. Find the helping verb that goes with the number.**

2. **Roll the die again. Find the action verb that goes with the number.**

Helping Verbs	Action Verbs
1. do	1. look
2. does	2. escape
3. does not	3. fly
4. can	4. run
5. might	5. search
6. may	6. hide

3. **Say a sentence with the action verb and helping verb. The first player to use all 6 action verbs and helping verbs in sentences correctly wins.**

Thinking Map

Creature Features

Use a comparison chart to compare animals and their features.

Features	Creature 1	Creature 2

Tell a partner how the animals are alike.

Going to the Zoo

Grammar Rules Verb: *to be*		
Verbs should match the subjects they are telling about.		
For yourself, use	**am**	*I **am** a shark. I'm hungry!*
For one other person or thing, use	**is**	*A fish **is** my prey. It's tasty.*
For someone you're talking to, yourself and others, or more than one person or thing, use	**are**	*You **are** interesting.* *My friend and I **are** here.* *The tiger's teeth **are** sharp.*

Write the correct form of the verb be to complete each sentence.

1. I _____ *am* _____ happy!

2. We _____ at the zoo.

3. That elephant _____ very big.

4. The young elephants _____ cute.

5. The tiger _____ hungry.

6. You _____ too close to the cage!

▬▬ **Read each sentence to a partner.**

Name _____   Date _____

"Living Lights"

Listen as your teacher reads. Follow with your finger.

1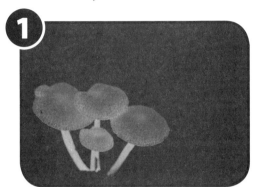

Living things use light to survive. Some mushrooms use light to attract insects. The insects spread the mushroom spores. A spore is like a seed.

2

Some animals use light to catch other animals. Glowworms use light to catch insects in their sticky threads. Then they eat the insects.

3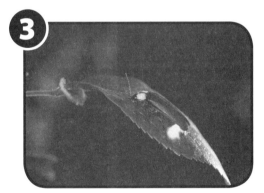

Some animals use light to send messages. Fireflies flash lights to find each other.

4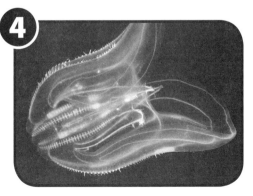

Some ocean animals use light to escape from predators. Bioluminescent animals are hard to see in bright water.

© Cengage Learning, Inc.

Sentence Building

Make sentences using different subjects.

1. Take turns with a partner.

2. Toss a marker onto the game board.

3. Make a sentence for the subject you land on. Use the correct form of **have**.

I	They	It
Animals	The insect	The scientist
We	You	Light

"Living Lights"

Use a comparison chart to compare bioluminescent animals.

How it uses light	Animal
to attract prey	glowworm anglerfish
to send messages	
to hide	

Use your comparison chart to tell a partner about the animals in "Living Lights."

Phonics Practice

Trigraphs: *thr, shr, squ*

throw   shrub   squid

Draw a line from the correct trigraph to the rest of the word. Write the word on the line.

1.	thr shr ink squ _____	**2.**	thr shr are squ _____
3.	thr shr ead squ _____	**4.**	thr shr irrel squ _____
5.	thr shr ed squ _____	**6.**	thr shr one squ _____

Work with a partner. Take turns reading the sentence and pointing to the objects.

Find a throne, a square, and a squirrel.

Name _____ Date _____

"Living Lights"

Use this passage to practice reading with proper phrasing.

Sometimes insects carry spores to new places.   7

Light attracts insects.   10

When they land on the glowing mushrooms,   17

some spores might stick to them.   23

When the insects leave, so do the spores!   31

From "Living Lights," page 118

Phrasing

B ☐ Rarely pauses while reading the text.   A ☐ Frequently pauses at appropriate points in the text.

I ☐ Occasionally pauses while reading the text.   AH ☐ Consistently pauses at all appropriate points in the text.

Accuracy and Rate Formula

Use the formula below to measure a reader's accuracy and rate while reading aloud.

_____ – _____ = _____
words attempted   number of errors   words correct per minute
in one minute   (wcpm)

Respond and Extend

Compare Genres

Use a comparison chart to compare "Living Lights" and "Clever Creatures."

Text features	"Living Lights"	"Clever Creatures"
is about animals	✓	✓
includes words that rhyme		✓
has facts		
has photographs		
has illustrations		

Work with a partner. Read each feature and see if it is in "Living Lights" and "Clever Creatures." Make a check if you see the feature.

Grammar

Insects at the Zoo

Grammar Rules Verbs: *to be* and *to have*

Verbs should match who or what they are telling about.

For yourself, use	**am**	*I **am** a scientist.*
	have	*I **have** work to do.*
For one other person or thing, use	**is**	*The Io moth **is** very clever.*
	has	*It **has** wings that look like big eyes.*
For someone you're talking to, yourself and others, or more than one person or thing, use	**are**	*These wings **are** a clever trick.*
	have	*Many moths **have** features that keep them safe.*

Choose the correct verb. Then read the sentence to a partner.

1. My teacher _____is_____ interested in all kinds of insects.
        is/are

2. He _____ good news for our class.
        has/have

3. We _____ going to the zoo on Friday!
        is/are

4. The zoo _____ a special place to see insects.
        has/have

5. I _____ excited about the trip to the zoo.
        am/is

6. You _____ invited to come, too!
        is/are

Writing Project

Ideas

Writing is well-developed when the message is clear and interesting to the reader. It is supported by details that show the writer knows the topic well.

	Is the message clear and focused?	Do the details show the writer knows the topic?
4 Wow!	❑ All of the writing is clear and focused.	❑ All the details tell about the topic. ❑ The writer knows the topic well.
3 Ahh.	❑ Most of the writing is clear and focused.	❑ Most of the details are about the topic. ❑ The writer knows the topic fairly well.
2 Hmm.	❑ Some of the writing is not clear. The writing lacks some focus.	❑ Some details are about the topic. ❑ The writer doesn't know the topic well.
1 Huh?	❑ The writing is not clear or focused.	❑ Many details are not about the topic. ❑ The writer does not know the topic.

Name _____ Date _____

Comparison Chart

Complete the comparison chart for your article.

My article is about _____ and _____.

Group	Facts, details, and examples
	• •
	• •
	• •

Writing Project

Revise

Use revision marks to make changes to this paragraph. Look for:

- a topic sentence
- relevant details

Revision Marks	
∧	Add
ꝰ	Take out
⬭⤻	Move to here

I like tree frogs and moths. They can protect themselves.

Some moths are brown like tree bark. Hungry birds can't see them.

Birds are very pretty. Tree frogs can blend into green leaves and

branches. They have tiny feet, too.

Edit and Proofread

Use revision marks to edit and proofread this paragraph. Look for:

- **subject-verb agreement**
- **correct use of apostrophes in contractions**
- **correct spelling of compound words**

Revision Marks	
^	Add
℘	Take out
⬭⤳	Move to here
⌣	Delete space

Fish protect themselves in different ways. Minnows swims

in big schools. Bigger fish ca'nt catch them. Some fish hides in side

poisonous plants. Bigger fish do'nt wants to eat them. Some fish

are the same color as rocks or plants. They can blend into the

bacground. Fish is amazing!

Unit Concept Map

Water for Everyone

Make a concept map with the answers to the Big Question:
Where do we get water?

Where do we get water?

Where does water go?

Problem and Solution

Fill out a problem-and-solution chart.

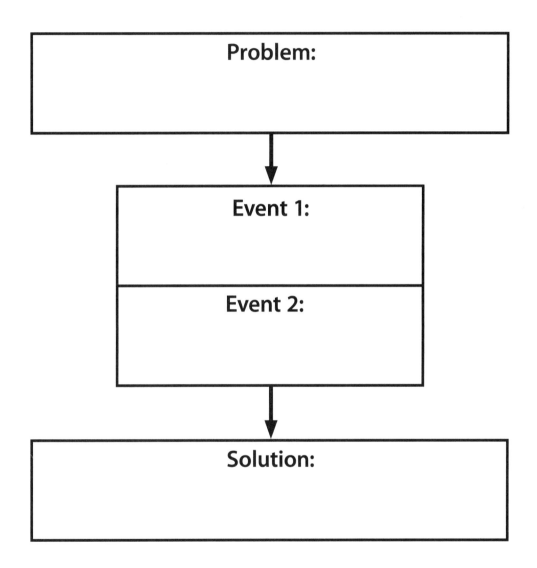

Problem:

Event 1:

Event 2:

Solution:

Tell a partner about a problem you solved.

Name _____ Date _____

A Rainy Weekend

Grammar Rules Adjectives

An **adjective** describes, or tells about, a noun.

What a person or thing is like	Size, color, and shape	"How many" or "how much"
loud	tiny	three
icy	white	a lot
scary	round	a little

Read the paragraph and categorize the adjectives.

Emma was <u>excited</u>. Her class was planning a <u>great</u> trip for Monday. But on Friday, <u>many</u> clouds rolled in. Soon, a <u>huge</u> storm started. It was still <u>rainy</u> on Saturday. On Sunday, the <u>yellow</u> sun appeared. On Monday, only <u>a few</u> puddles were left. The <u>icy</u> storm was over. The trip would be <u>fun</u>!

What a person or thing is like	Size, color, and shape	"How many" or "how much"
excited		

◀ Tell a partner about a storm you have seen. Use adjectives.

Name _____ Date _____

"Frog Brings Rain"

Listen as your teacher reads. Follow with your finger.

1

Fire is moving to the First People's homes. Cardinal warns First Woman. First Man tells First Woman that Water will put out Fire.

2

First Woman makes a bottle and fills it with Water. Robin carries it to Fire. There isn't enough water to put Fire out. First Woman asks for help, but nobody will help her.

3

Finally, First Woman asks Frog to help. He soaks up Water in his coat. Then White Crane carries Frog over Fire. Water falls from Frog's coat as Rain. Water puts out Fire.

To this day, Frog lives in this swamp. He brings Rain with his song.

Grammar

Animal Mix-Up

Play a guessing game with a partner.

---

1. Choose a word from each column.

2. Act out the animal for a partner.

3. Your partner gets:
   - 1 point for guessing the animal
   - 1 point for guessing the adjective

4. Exchange roles.

5. The student with the most points wins.

Article	Adjective	Animal
a	angry	bear
an	brave	beaver
the	excited	crane
	friendly	fish
	huge	frog
	quiet	snail

Vocabulary

Vocabulary Bingo

Play Bingo using the Key Words from this unit.

Name ______________________ Date ______________

Reread and Retell

"Frog Brings Rain"

Use a problem-and-solution chart to tell about "Frog Brings Rain."

Problem:

First Woman needs Water to put out Fire.

Event 1:

She asks Hunting People to take Water to Fire.

Event 2:

Solution:

Use your chart to tell a partner how First Woman and Frog solve the problem.

Phonics Practice

Long e spelled *ie, ey*

chi<u>e</u>f   ke<u>y</u>

Read each word. Circle the word that goes with each picture.

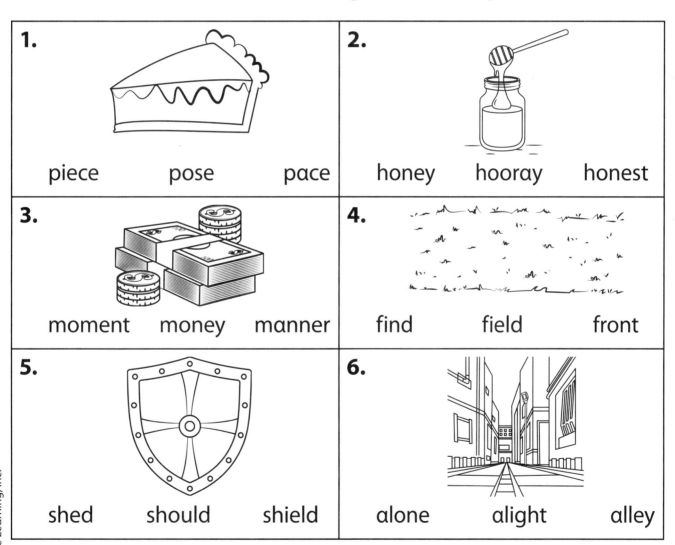

1. piece pose pace	**2.** honey hooray honest
3. moment money manner	**4.** find field front
5. shed should shield	**6.** alone alight alley

Work with a partner. Take turns reading the sentence.

I can buy a piece of honey cake with money.

Fluency

"Frog Brings Rain"

Use this passage to practice reading with proper expression.

On the east side, it fell as white rain. On the   11

west side, it was yellow rain.   17

Water put out Fire. Then Frog and Crane   25

returned home.   27

From "Frog Brings Rain," page 164

Expression

B ☐ Does not read with feeling.   A ☐ Reads with appropriate feeling for most content.

I ☐ Reads with some feeling, but it does not match   AH ☐ Reads with appropriate feeling for all content.
content.

Accuracy and Rate Formula

Use the formula below to measure a reader's accuracy and rate while reading aloud.

_____ − _____ = _____
words attempted   number of errors   words corrected per
in one minute   minute (wcpm)

Compare Explanations

Show how the two explanations for rain are different.

How is rain made?	
Traditional tale explanation	**Science experiment explanation**
• Frog carries water.	• Warm, wet air rises.

💬 **Ask a partner questions about the story and the science experiment.**

Grammar

After the Storm

Grammar Rules Adjectives and Articles

Adjectives and articles can come before nouns.

An **adjective** can describe what a noun is like.	Examples: A **light** rain starts to fall. The raindrops feel **icy** and **cold**.
An **article** can tell which noun you mean.	Examples: **A** cloud fills up with water. Raindrops fall on **the** green hill. It is **an** amazing thing to see.

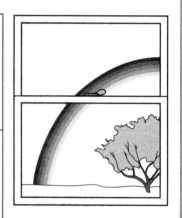

Read the passage and add adjectives and articles.

The storm lasted for ___three___ days. Then the _____ sun rose. It dried up the _____ grass. _____ puddles started to disappear. Then we looked up into the _____ sky. There was _____ amazing rainbow. It looked _____ and _____. Soon the weather was _____ and _____ again.

Tell a partner about weather you like. Use adjectives and articles.

Thinking Map

Cause and Effect

Fill out a cause-and-effect chart to show what happened when you did something.

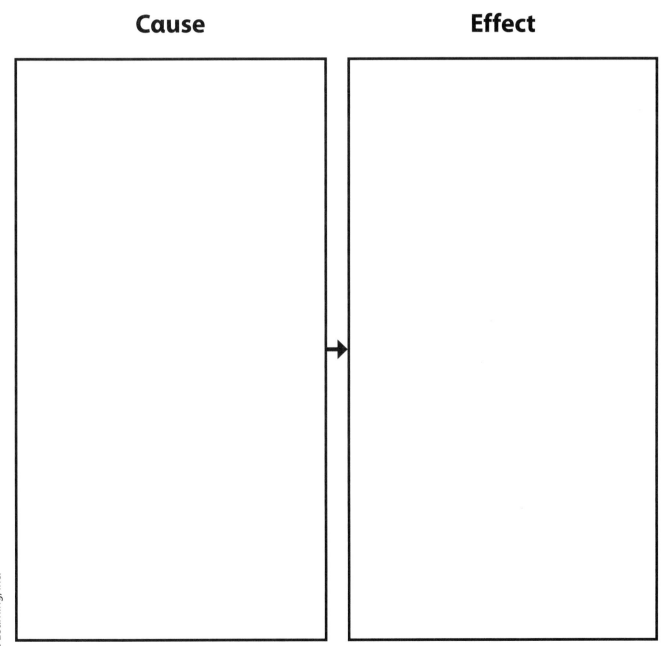

Cause	Effect

Tell a partner about what happened and why.

Grammar

Going to the Lake

Grammar Rules Adverbs with *-ly*

Adverbs tell about actions. Many adverbs tell **how** something happens. These adverbs usually end in **-ly**.

Examples: *The sun rose* **slow**<u>**ly**</u>.

Anna got up **quick**<u>**ly**</u>.

Read the adverbs in the box. Write the adverb that will correctly complete each sentence. Then read each sentence to a partner.

| proudly | loudly | softly | brightly | quickly | safely |

1. The sun shines _____*brightly*_____ in the sky.

2. "Are you ready to go?" Mom whispered _____ .

3. "YES!" Anna yelled _____ .

4. "I remembered to pack my life vest," Anna said _____ .

5. "The vest will help me swim _____ ," Anna added.

6. Mom and Anna packed the car _____ and took off.

Name _____   Date _____

Key Points Reading

"PlayPumps: Turning Work into Play"

Listen as your teacher reads. Follow with your finger.

1

Everyone needs water to drink, cook, and clean. Some countries have a lot of clean water. In other countries, clean water is hard to find.

2

A new invention is bringing water to parts of Africa. Children play on the PlayPump. As the PlayPump spins, it pumps clean water from under the ground. The water goes into a water tank. The tank holds water for the community.

3

Now getting clean water is fast, easy, and fun. The pumps bring water to almost two million people.

Grammar

When Did It Happen?

Grammar Rules Adverbs That Tell When

Some **adverbs** tell **when** something happens.

Examples: **Years ago** we got a water pump.

Last week our water pump broke.

Then we ran out of water.

Today we fixed the pump.

Read the sentences. Circle the adverbs that tell when.

1. (Years ago) people in some parts of the world did not have water.

2. Then someone came up with the idea of PlayPumps.

3. Now PlayPumps help bring water to many towns.

4. Children often play and make the pumps work.

5. Many more people have water today.

Write a sentence about when you last drank some water. Remember to use an adverb that tells when. Share your sentence with a partner.

_____

_____

© Cengage Learning, Inc.

Reread and Retell

"PlayPumps: Turning Work into Play"

Use a cause-and-effect chart to tell about "PlayPumps: Turning Work into Play."

Cause	Effect
Kids ride on the PlayPump and turn the wheel.	

Use your chart to tell a partner about more causes and effects in "PlayPumps: Turning Work into Play."

Phonics Practice

Vowel Sounds and Spellings: *or, ore*

c<u>or</u>n   sh<u>ore</u>

Read each word. Circle the word that goes with each picture.

1. house horse his	**2.** fern fork find
3. stork strike stir	**4.** care cane core
5. hole horn home	**6.** snare snap snore

Work with a partner. Take turns reading the sentence and pointing to the objects.

Find a stork, a horse, and a fork.

© Cengage Learning, Inc.

Fluency

"PlayPumps: Turning Work into Play"

Use this passage to practice reading with proper intonation.

PlayPumps are made in South Africa. Today,	7
there are more than 1,200 PlayPumps in	14
use. They bring water to almost two million	22
people.	23

From "PlayPumps," page 196

Intonation

B	☐ Does not change pitch	A	☐ Changes pitch to match some of the content
I	☐ Changes pitch, but does not match content	AH	☐ Changes pitch to match all the content

Accuracy and Rate Formula

Use the formula below to measure a reader's accuracy and rate while reading aloud.

$$\underline{\qquad\qquad} \; - \; \underline{\qquad\qquad} \; = \; \underline{\qquad\qquad}$$

words attempted in one minute	number of errors	words correct per minute (wcpm)

Name _____   Date _____

"The Mighty Colorado"

Listen to your teacher and mark your answers in the **planner** below.

❶ What is the author's purpose for writing?

☐ to tell a story   **OR**   ☐ to give information

☐ to entertain

❷ What is your purpose for reading?

☐ for enjoyment   **OR**   ☐ for information

❸ What type of story are you going to read?

☐ fiction   **OR**   ☐ nonfiction

To read fiction:	**To read nonfiction:**
• Identify the characters.	• Read more slowly.
• Think about what happens and when it happens.	• Identify facts about real people or events.
• Use what you know to read new words.	• Use maps, diagrams, and photographs.
	• Concentrate as you read.

© Cengage Learning, Inc.

Name _____ Date _____

Compare Information

Use a comparison chart to compare "PlayPumps: Turning Work into Play" and "The Mighty Colorado."

How people get water	
"PlayPumps: Turning Work into Play"	**"The Mighty Colorado"**
• Kids play.	

 Share your chart with a partner. Take turns asking questions about the information.

Grammar

Adverb Tic-Tac-Toe

1. Play with a partner.
2. Player X chooses and reads the sentence. Player Y tells if the adverb tells how or when.
3. Player Y marks the square if the answer is correct.
4. Players switch roles and take turns to see which player is the first to get three marks in a row.

The water stopped <u>yesterday</u>.	We <u>quickly</u> called the plumber.	The plumber arrived <u>soon</u>.
The plumber worked <u>carefully</u> to find the clog.	She <u>finally</u> found the clog.	<u>Then</u> she cleared it up.
<u>Slowly</u> the water began to flow.	We have plenty of water <u>today</u>.	We <u>gladly</u> fill our water jugs.

© Cengage Learning, Inc.

Writing Project

Voice

Every writer has a special way of saying things, or a voice. The voice should sound genuine, or real, and be unique to that writer.

	Does the tone, formal or informal, fit the purpose and audience?	Does the writing sound genuine to the writer?
4 Wow!	❑ The writer's tone fits the purpose and audience.	❑ The writing is genuine. It shows who the writer is.
3 Ahh.	❑ The writer's tone mostly fits the purpose and audience.	❑ Most of the writing sounds genuine.
2 Hmm.	❑ Some of the writing fits the purpose and audience. Some does not.	❑ Some of the writing sounds genuine.
1 Huh?	❑ The writer's tone does not fit the purpose and audience.	❑ The writing does not sound genuine.

Problem-and-Solution Chart

Complete the problem-and-solution chart for your folk tale.

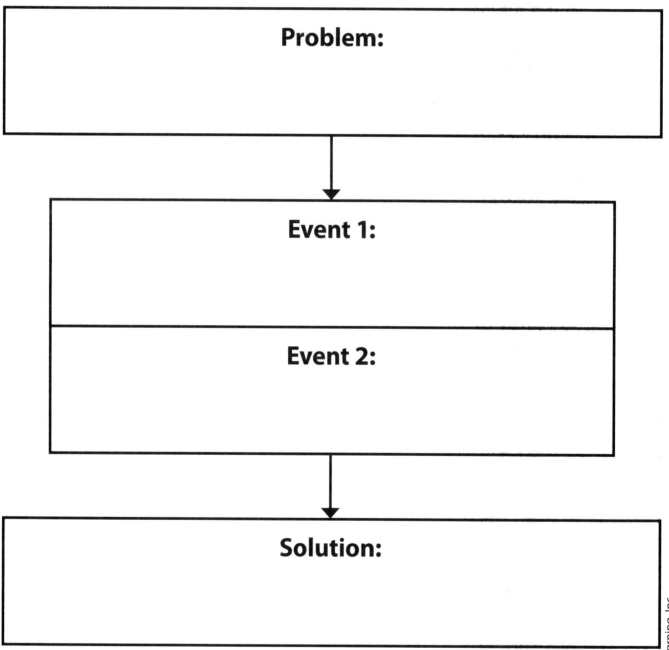

Problem:

Event 1:

Event 2:

Solution:

Writing Project

Revise

Use revision marks to make changes to the paragraph. Look for:

- a clear description of the problem
- a unique voice
- precise words

Revision Marks	
∧	Add
℘	Take out
⬭⤴	Move to here

Ocean was sad. Ocean wanted friends. Everyone was scared

of Ocean. Ocean stopped making waves. A boy saw no waves.

He said, "Look!" Everyone went in.

Edit and Proofread

Use revision marks to edit and proofread these paragraphs. Look for:

- **adjectives used correctly**
- **adverbs with -ly**
- **dialogue with quotation marks**

Revision Marks	
∧	Add
℘	Take out
⬭↰	Move to here
⬭	Check spelling
"Or"	Insert quotation mark

"I am lonely, said Ocean. Ocean's waves crashed loudly on the

sand. Ocean saw that the loudly waves scared people.

Sudden Ocean yelled, Wait! I have an idea!" Ocean made her

waves smaller and quieter. Then a little boy ran in and swam.

Other people went in, too.

"I am not lonely anymore," said Ocean happyly.

Unit Concept Map

Lend a Hand

**Make a concept map with the answers to the Big Question:
What are our responsibilities to each other?**

What are our
responsibilities
to each other?

Thinking Map

Character Traits

Make a character map about two characters you know.

Character	What the character does	What the character is like

> Tell a partner which character was your favorite and why.

Grammar

Helping Out

Grammar Rules Parts of a Sentence

A sentence has a <u>naming part</u> and a <u>telling part</u>.
The naming part usually comes before the telling part.

Example: <u>*The children*</u> <u>*work together*</u>.

Naming part   Telling part

Circle the naming parts. Underline the telling parts.

1. (Majid and Amy) <u>start the meeting</u>.

2. Everyone wants to clean up the school.

3. The teachers put trash bins around the yard.

4. The children pick up trash.

5. The school looks much better.

 Use the naming part of one sentence to make a new sentence. Share your sentence with a partner.

"Aesop's Fables"

Listen as your teacher reads. Follow with your finger.

1

A mouse wakes a sleeping lion. He traps her under his paw. She begs him to let her go because she might be able to help him someday. The lion thinks it's a silly idea, but he lets her go.

2

Hunters trap the lion in a net. The mouse chews through the net and sets the lion free.
Moral: Great help can come from small friends.

3

Farmer Bean finds an eagle stuck in a mousetrap and sets it free.

4

Later, the farmer is eating beside a wall. The eagle takes his hat. He chases the eagle. It drops his hat. He goes back, but the wall has fallen down!
Moral: Help can come from unexpected places.

Grammar

Friends in Need

Grammar Rules Sentence Punctuation

- Every sentence begins with a **capital letter**:
  Example: *Fables teach lessons about life.*

- Every sentence ends with an end mark like a **period**:
  Example: *They are fun to read.*

Write each sentence correctly. Use a capital letter and a period.

1. a farmer hears a cry in the barn

A farmer hears a cry in the barn.

2. he frees an eagle from a trap

_____

3. the eagle takes his hat

_____

4. a wall tumbles down

_____

5. the farmer is grateful

_____

Write a complete sentence about one of the fables. Read it to a partner.

"Aesop's Fables"

Make a character map to describe the characters in "Aesop's Fables."

Character	What the character does	What the character is like
the lion	lets the mouse leave	generous
Farmer Bean		

Use your character map to tell a partner about the characters in "Aesop's Fables."

Vowel Sounds and Spellings: ear, eer

beard

deer

Read each word. Write the word that completes each sentence.

---

1. We _____ at the game.

chair
chore
cheer

2. I had a _____ on my face.

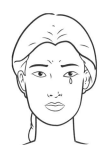

tear
tore
tar

3. I have two _____.

earns
ores
ears

4. The driver will _____ the car.

stair
store
steer

Work with a partner. Take turns reading and answering the question.

Do you cover your ears when everyone cheers?

Fluency

"Aesop's Fables"

Use this passage to practice reading with proper expression.

"Ah!" said the lion. "But you will make a tasty　　　10

snack."　　　11

"No, no!" the mouse pleaded. "What will my　　　19

babies do if you eat me?"　　　25

From "Aesop's Fables," page 226

Expression

| B | ☐ Does not read with feeling. | A | ☐ Reads with appropriate feeling for most content. |
| I | ☐ Reads with some feeling, but does not match content. | AH | ☐ Reads with appropriate feeling for all content. |

Accuracy and Rate Formula

Use the formula to measure a reader's accuracy and rate while reading aloud.

$$\underline{\hspace{3cm}} - \underline{\hspace{3cm}} = \underline{\hspace{3cm}}$$

| words attempted in one minute | number of errors | words correct per minute (wcpm) |

Name _____   Date _____

"Wisdom of the Ages"

Use a reflection journal as you read the proverbs.

Page	Proverb	My connection

▸ Tell a partner why a proverb has special meaning for you.

Compare Settings and Plots

Use a comparison chart to compare the plots and settings of the two fables by Aesop.

Title	Setting	Plot
"The Lion and the Mouse"	takes place in the forest	
"The Farmer and the Eagle"		

Share your comparison chart with a partner to talk about the fables.

Grammar

Build a Sentence Game

1. Play with a partner.

2. Toss a coin onto one of the sentence parts below.

3. Put it together with another sentence part to make a complete sentence.

4. Your partner takes a turn.

5. The player who makes the most complete sentences wins.

My friends	make good choices.
are thoughtful.	The teachers
My classmates	give to others.
help me study.	Mom and Dad
Our cousins	show respect.

Name _____   Date _____

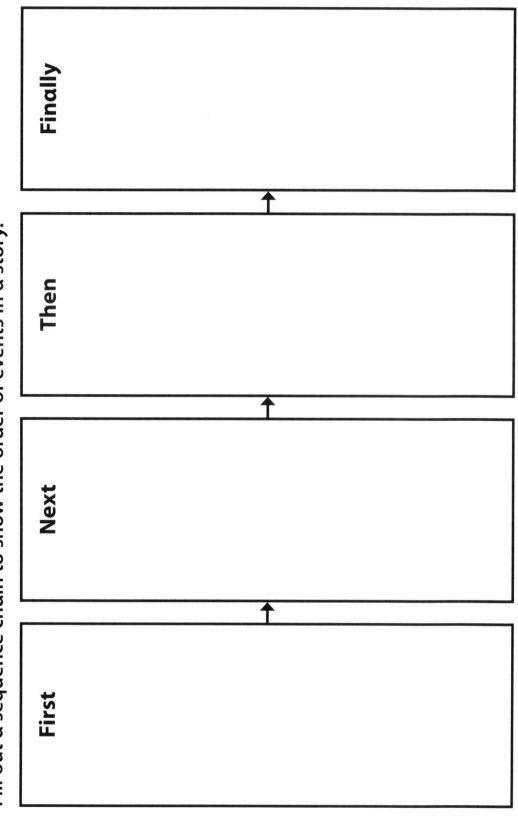

Thinking Map

Sequence

Fill out a sequence chain to show the order of events in a story.

First	Next	Then	Finally

Use the sequence chain to tell the story to a partner.

Grammar

Volunteers

Grammar Rules Subjects

Every sentence has a naming part and a telling part. The **subject** is the naming part. It tells who or what the sentence is about.

Example: ***The doctor*** *saves many lives.*

subject

Circle the subject in each sentence.

1. Volunteers help others.

2. They aid people in need.

3. Some people pick up trash.

4. Others give away food.

5. Everyone makes a difference.

 Change the subject of a sentence to make a new sentence. Share your new sentence with a partner.

"Giving Back"

Listen as your teacher reads. Follow with your finger.

1 William Allard is a photographer. While driving in Peru, he saw a boy named Eduardo. He was crying. A driver had killed his sheep. Eduardo was responsible for the sheep. Allard took a picture of Eduardo and his sheep.

2 A magazine printed the picture. Readers sent money. An organization used the money to buy more sheep for Eduardo. It built a water pump for his village. The rest of the money helped children in Peru go to school.

3 Allard's pictures have entertained people, but this one picture made someone's life better.

Happy to Help

Grammar Rules Predicates

Every sentence has a naming part and a telling part. The **predicate** is the telling part. It tells what the subject does.

Example: *The leader <u>decided on a plan</u>*.
predicate

Underline the predicate in each sentence.

I <u>want to help others</u>. My family serves food to the poor. My generous friend comes to help. She gives money for food. Together, we feed many people. We both feel happy to help others.

With a partner, change one of the predicates to make a new sentence.

Reread and Retell

"Giving Back"

Fill out a sequence chain to show the order of events in "Giving Back."

First	Next	Then	Finally
William Allard sees a boy crying because his sheep have died.			

Tell a partner about the events in sequence.

Phonics Practice

Vowel Sounds and Spellings: ar

car   shark

Read each word. Circle the word that goes with the picture.

1. jeer jar jam	**2.** march mend mound
3. her horn harp	**4.** large last leap
5. shape sharp shave	**6.** scrap skirt scarf

Work with a partner. Take turns reading the sentence and pointing to the objects.

Find a scarf, a harp, and a jar.

Fluency

"Giving Back"

Use this passage to practice reading with correct phrasing.

When I got back to my hotel,   7

I thought a lot about Eduardo.   13

I thought about his broken sheep   19

and his tears.   22

I thought about his family.   27

I realized what it meant   32

to lose that many sheep.   37

The mountains of Peru   41

can be a hard place to live and work.   50

From "Giving Back," page 260

Phrasing

B ☐ Rarely pauses while reading the text.   A ☐ Frequently pauses at appropriate points in the text.

I ☐ Occasionally pauses while reading the text.   AH ☐ Consistently pauses at all appropriate points in the text.

Accuracy and Rate Formula

Use the formula to measure a reader's accuracy and rate while reading aloud.

_____ − _____ = _____
words attempted   number of errors   words correct per minute
 in one minute   (wcpm)

Name _____   Date _____

"The Water Hero"

Complete a dialogue journal with a partner as you read
"The Water Hero."

What I think	What my partner thinks
Page _____ _____ _____ _____ _____	_____ _____ _____ _____
Page _____ _____ _____ _____ _____	_____ _____ _____ _____
Page _____ _____ _____ _____ _____	_____ _____ _____ _____

Talk with your partner about your ideas and opinions.

Respond and Extend

Compare Author's Purpose

Work with a partner to fill in the comparison chart.

Author's Purpose	William Allard	Anna Goy
to persuade		
to inform		✓
to entertain		
to share experiences	✓	
to tell about other parts of the world		
to motivate		

_____ **Which selection did you like best? Share your opinion with a partner.**

Grammar

Do We Agree?

Grammar Rules Subject-Verb Agreement

Every sentence has two parts: the **subject** and the <u>verb</u>.
The subject and verb must agree.

Example: ***The boy*** <u>*waits*</u>.

one person

Example: ***Parents*** <u>*smile*</u>.

more than one person

1. Play with a partner.

2. Point to a subject card.

3. Your partner points to a verb card.

4. If the subject and verb agree, cross out both cards.

5. Play until all the cards are crossed out.

Subject Cards			
Avi	Teresa	Mr. and Mrs. Mendez	You and I
He	She	They	We

Verb Cards			
wants	builds	helps	hopes
work	study	need	carry

Ideas

Writing is well-developed when the message is clear and interesting to the reader. It is supported by details that show the writer knows the topic well.

	Is the message clear and focused?	**Do the details show the writer knows the topic?**
4 Wow!	❑ All of the writing is clear and focused.	❑ All the details are about the topic. ❑ The writer knows the topic well.
3 Ahh.	❑ Most of the writing is clear and focused.	❑ Most of the details are about the topic. ❑ The writer knows the topic fairly well.
2 Hmm.	❑ Some of the writing is not clear. The writing lacks some focus.	❑ Some details are about the topic. ❑ The writer doesn't know the topic well.
1 Huh?	❑ The writing is not clear or focused.	❑ Many details are not about the topic. ❑ The writer does not know the topic.

Sequence Chain

Complete a sequence chain to show the steps that led to a good deed being done.

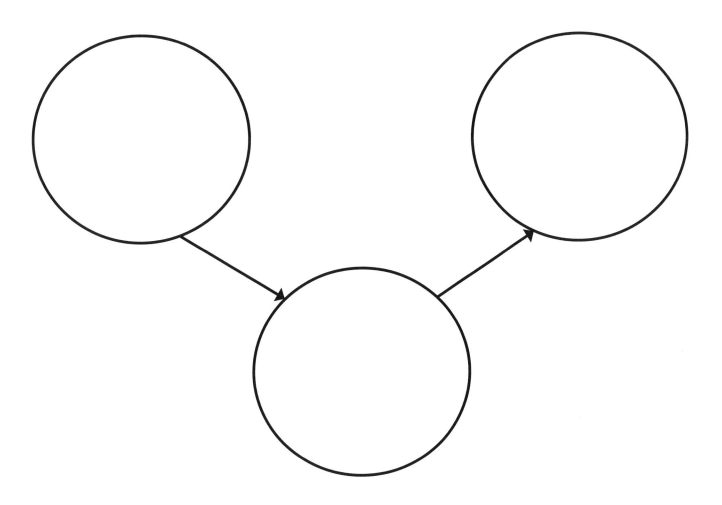

Writing Project

Revise

Use revision marks to make changes to this interview. Look for:

- **good questions**
- **the best details**

Revision Marks	
^	Add
℘	Take out
⌒⟶	Move to here

Brad Nguyen: Volunteer at Our Local Library

Brad Nguyen started a children's reading group at the library.

I wanted to know why and how he started the group.

Why did you start the group? I want to help kids enjoy reading.

I read fantasies.

How do you get to the library? I ride my bike.

How did you start the group? I told the librarian I could read on

Saturdays. She liked my plan. She helped me start the group.

When I'm done, I go play basketball.

Edit and Proofread

Use revision marks to edit and
proofread this interview. Look for:

- complete sentences
- question marks
- a prefix

Revision Marks	
∧	Add
ﻭ	Take out
⬭⌒	Move to here
⬭SP	Check spelling

Isabel Vega: Community Helper

Isabel Vega delivers meals to her neighbors. I talked to her about

the home-delivery program and its benefits.

Why did you start delivering meals? My neighbor broke her leg

because of a mistep. I wanted to help.

How often do you deliver meals I deliver meals three or four

times a week. The program really helps people who are unable to

prepare meals for themselves.

Do you enjoys delivering meals? Yes, it's fun. I get to visit with

a lot of people.

Photographic Credits

1.3 FatCamera/Getty Images. 1.14 (t) 4X5 Collection/SuperStock. (c) FRILET Patrick/AGE Fotostock. (b) MediaProduction/Getty Images. 2.14 (t) Thomas Marent/Minden Pictures/Getty Images. (tc) Steve Percival/ Science Source. (bc) Atsuo Fujimaru/Minden Pictures. (b) Dimijian Greg/Science Source/Getty Images. 3.14 (b) Roundabout water solutions. (t) Bartosz Hadyniak/Getty Images. 4.3 Fuse/Getty Images. 4.14 (t) Willliam Albert Allard/National Geographic Image Collection. (b) William Albert Allard/National Geographic Image Collection. (c) Willliam Albert Allard/National Geographic Image Collection.